Martin Luther: Justified by Grace

By Carter Lindberg

Contents

1. The Reformation Context:
   A Crisis in Values 2

2. "Let God be God"—The Clue
   to Luther's Life and Ministry 14

3. The Rocky Road of Reformation . . 24

4. The Christian Life:
   Word and Sacraments 34

5. The Christian Life:
   Being Christ to the Neighbor 44

6. The Reception of Luther 54

1

The Reformation Context: A Crisis in Values

"Little crooks are hanged; big crooks govern our lands and cities."[1] This statement is not a cynical line from an editorial concerning the most recent Wall Street or Washington scandal. Rather, these are the words of Reynard the Fox from the medieval animal epic of the same name. Reynard goes on to explain his dishonesty and immorality to his nephew, Grimbert the Badger: "Sometimes I think that, since everybody does it, this is the way it ought to be."[2] The fable ends with the moral, "Money counts, and nothing else."[3] Reynard's point is that people who want to get to the top should imitate him.

This was the world into which Martin Luther (1483–1546) was born, a world not unlike our own. It was a world where the strong took advantage of the weak. It was a world experiencing one catastrophe after another. It was a world of plague, famine, war, and death, graphically depicted by the artist Albrecht Dürer (Luther's contemporary) in his *Four Horsemen of the Apocalypse*. It was also a world undergoing rapid and puzzling social change due to technological developments, urban growth, and the displacement of the feudal economy by capitalism.

In the midst of all these crises and radical changes, the old morality no longer made much sense. To make matters even worse, the church was still reacting only to its own internal crises and seemed to many people to be more a part of the problem than a source of hope.

A World in Crisis

Luther's world was in crisis. But what is a crisis? In medicine a crisis is a change that indicates whether the patient will recover or die. Historians use the word *crisis* to refer to a decisive moment or turning point in a society. A description of the many factors we listed above may help us understand why we refer to the crisis of the late Middle Ages as a crisis of values or as a crisis of faith.

Fourteenth-century Europe experienced an extended food crisis that left many people too weak to resist the plague. As a result, whole cities and regions were ghost areas by the end of the century. Because of famine, plague, and feudal warfare, life expectancy· was about forty years. The time of life that we have the luxury of referring to as a "mid-life crisis" was to the medieval person old age.

By the late fifteenth century the population had recovered from the ravages of famine and plague, but people were still feeling the social effects. Many peasants had left the devastated areas and had moved to the cities and towns. These people hoped to make better lives for themselves there. This flight from the rural areas jeopardized the livelihood of the landowners who took whatever steps they could to keep their workers on the farms. In many cases these steps were quite oppressive. Serfdom was established, or it was strengthened where it was already in existence. A movement was also underway to replace local laws and customs with Roman law in order to squeeze as much labor and as many goods as possible out of peasants and day laborers. The ecclesiastical landlords were particularly adept at this practice because they were already familiar with Roman law in the form of canon law. This behavior was one of the reasons for the widespread anticlerical anger that existed on the eve of the Reformation.

Those peasants who were able to move to the cities discovered they were not welcome. They were excluded from the guilds, the medieval equivalent to modern professions and building trades. These people were almost always excluded from citizenship. If they found work, it was generally as day laborers subject to the whims of whoever hired them. Since laborers had no "safety net" of social security or savings, they were always on the edge of poverty. They fell over that narrow edge when work was unavailable. Some experts have estimated that seventy-five percent of the population suffered severe nutritional deficiencies, poor clothing, and miserable housing. As a result, outbreaks of peasant violence, culminating in the Peasants' War of 1524–25, occurred. But few of the well-to-do members of society were sensitive to the causes of these outbreaks of rage.

As we all know too well, city life takes money. The late medieval cities were growing because they were becoming the places where early capitalism could thrive. That situation made cities attractive to outsiders who hoped to make their fortune there. But this new money economy was as unsettling as it was attractive. Instead of trading goods that a neighbor crafted or grew, people found themselves in an impersonal situation of exchanging money for something from a stranger. And, of course, with enough money anything could be had—privileges, positions, prostitutes, and even penance to make people feel better about whatever they had bought! But the city and money combination did not make everyone feel better; it left many people feeling uneasy and guilty. The traditional morality was incapable of dealing with this insecurity because, as canon law stated, "A merchant is rarely or never able to please God."[4]

Technological developments also stimulated the insecurities of the age. The invention of movable metal type, inexpensive paper, and good ink led to a media explosion. More books were printed between 1460 and 1500 than scribes and monks had produced throughout the entire Middle Ages. The development of sump pumps and smelting led to a boom in mining and metallurgy. One effect of this boom was a five hundred percent increase in silver production. This increase in turn led to inflation because much of the silver was made into coins.

Another development was the invention of a stable gunpowder mixture, which encouraged the production of guns and cannon. Indiscriminate death and destruction were possible beyond the medieval person's wildest dreams. When this technology was coupled with national and religious fanaticism, these dreams became a devastating reality. But people could make a lot of money in the arms business, so this fledgling military-industrial complex grew and bore its deadly fruit.

Crisis in the Church

All these developments contributed to the insecurity that always accompanies rapid social change. What plunged this insecurity into profound social turmoil was the crisis affecting the late medieval church. By Luther's time the question was not whether but how and when the church would be reformed. The crisis was not just the result of the fact that corrupt and immoral persons held positions of leadership in the church. The institution itself was in crisis.

In the late fourteenth century a series of events led to the deposition of one pope and the election of another by the same legitimate College of Cardinals. The deposed pope refused to recognize the action against him; and for the first time in history there were two popes, each legitimately elected and each excommunicating the other. Efforts to rescue the papacy led at one point to three popes! The papacy, upon which Christians considered their salvation to be dependent, was itself in crisis. The church to which medieval society looked for guaranteed symbols of security was itself insecure. At the very time when medieval society faced unprecedented social anxieties, the credibility of the church was in grave doubt.

Due to the crisis of the church, the credibility of religion in every area of piety and theology was also in crisis. Scholars have sometimes puzzled over the fact that a surge of popular piety occurred in the late Middle Ages. Why does this era appear to be one of the most religious and devout periods in Western history? Perhaps the reason is that in times of crisis people tend to yearn for the "good old days" and try harder to imitate what they think those days were. The people of no other period in church history celebrated as many religious festivals and processions or threw themselves so wholeheartedly into the task of church construction as did the people of the late Middle Ages. Mass pilgrimages caught on like wildfire, frequently sparked by some perceived miracle and usually associated with the bread of the Lord's Supper. The dark side of this devotion erupted in mass attacks on Jews and supposed witches. Many innocent people suffered.

Miracles multiplied everywhere in the Empire. The veneration of saints reached its peak and changed its form. Saints were increasingly depicted life-size, individualized and garbed in contemporary dress. The saints were also aligned with the various social groupings and were made patrons for every human need. The practice of giving children saints' names became so widespread that the old German names all but disappeared. Insecure about salvation, people attempted to guarantee it by finding mediators between themselves and God.

Death seems never to have been more realistically considered than in this era and hardly ever so anxiously feared. Even today the bizarre paintings of Hieronymous Bosch fascinate us. Their rapid-breeding hybrid creatures were associated with lust and fertility but in the end symbolized sterility and death. Artistic realism also blossomed with popular manuals on the art of dying and depictions of the dance of death.

Relic collections abounded. Luther's contemporary, Cardinal Albrecht, believed his collection was worth 39,245,120 years off purgatory. The extraordinary success of the trade in indulgences was fueled as much by the desires of believers as by the financial interests of the church. Does this situation seem surprising? Think of the similar appeal and success of some of our modern media evangelists who promise to satisfy our desires to control God and to conquer insecurity. One scholar has characterized the late medieval period as having an immense appetite for the divine.

Theological and Pastoral Responses to Insecurity

The attempts of late medieval theology and pastoral practice to provide security in an insecure world only led to insecurity and uncertainty about salvation. One of the key ideas expressing the heart of this uncertainty about salvation was presented in the phrase *facere quod in se est*—do what lies within you. That is, if you strive to love God to the best of your ability, as weak as that may be, God will reward your efforts with the grace to do even better. God, the medieval theologians claimed, has made a covenant to be our contractual partner in creation and in salvation. In other words, medieval theology was reflecting the new social, economic, and political developments of the late medieval world.

In religion as in early capitalism, work merited reward. Individuals were to be responsible for their own life, society, and world on the basis and within the limits of the covenant God stipulated. The concern of the theologians was to provide an avenue of security for human beings through participation in the process of salvation. This approach was the theologians' response to the crises of the late medieval period. The result of this theology, however, was to enhance the crisis because it threw persons back on their own inadequate resources.

Perhaps an analogy will help clarify this covenant theology. Parents are often reluctant to make absolute

7

demands on their children. After all, popular literature frequently warns us not to ask so much of our
children that they become stifled and "uptight." We
are supposed to help them "realize themselves." On
the other hand, parents also recognize that life would
be equally frustrating if children were given no limits
and expectations. So, one common course parents
follow is to tell Johnny or Mary, "Your father and I do
not expect you to excel in everything. Just do the best
you can, and we will love you even though you do not
get straight A's and become class president or athlete
of the year." The intention is to provide guidelines but
avoid excessive pressure.

For some people such an approach may work just
fine. But for sensitive people such an approach creates
a great deal of insecurity because the question that
arises is, "How do I know when I have done my best?"
No matter what people accomplish in this framework,
they can easily think they could have done more with
just a little extra effort. In other words, the burden of
proof always falls back on the person.

"Do what lies within you." "Do the best you can."
These ideas are not really so strange to us. Some
people might even suggest that they exemplify the
American way of life: Realize your own potential;
anyone can be a success if he or she only tries hard
enough; you can better yourself. But how did this idea
enter medieval theology and worship?

This concept came from the classical Greek philoso-
pher Aristotle who, though not a Christian, had a
profound effect on the people of the Middle Ages. If
we look briefly at how the medieval theologians
applied just two of Aristotle's ideas, we can see how
influential he was.

In logic Aristotle posited that like is known by like.
Applied to theology, this concept means that fellowship with God can only take place when the sinner is
raised to likeness to God. The sinner must become
holy because God is holy and does not associate with
the unholy. To repeat, like is known by like. We may
see the influence of this idea if we ask, Where is

8

fellowship with God achieved? The answer can only be, On God's level. The sinner must become "like" God, that is, perfected and raised to where God is.

But how is the sinner to accomplish this feat? Aristotle's other idea comes into play at this point. Aristotle spoke of self-improvement in terms of what he called a *habitus*, a personal modification through practice. People acquire skills by practicing them. A person becomes a guitarist by practicing playing the guitar. A person becomes a good citizen by practicing civic virtues. A person becomes ethical by practicing moral virtues. Through such habits or practices one's ethics becomes a kind of second nature.

The medieval theologians took this basically common sense idea and applied it to acquiring righteousness before God. They "baptized" Aristotle's philosophy by saying that God through the sacraments infuses a supernatural "habit" in us. On the basis of this habitual grace, we are responsible for practicing this habit, developing it, and actualizing it. Insofar as we perfect the gifts God has given us, we merit more grace. Thomas Aquinas was fond of saying that grace does not do away with nature but perfects it. So, the famous scholastic phrase "do what lies within you" means that salvation is a process that takes place *within* us as we perfect ourselves. Put another way, we become righteous before God as we do righteous acts, as we do good works. But to an insecure and anxious person living in an insecure and anxious age, the question again becomes, "How do I know if I have done enough good works to merit salvation?"

The common answer in the Middle Ages took the form of what we might call the "Avis mentality"—try harder! This answer is the clue to that great surge in popular piety we mentioned earlier. People who doubted their salvation were encouraged to put more effort into striving to attain it. The church consciously stimulated this effort by emphasizing its translation of Ecclesiastes 9:1: "No one knows whether he is worthy of God's love or hate."

Luther's Response: The Certainty of God's Promise

Luther's response to the crisis of his time began with the recognition that the religious solution of trying harder to merit God's favor only compounded the problem. Indeed, Luther was convinced that whenever salvation is conceived in covenantal terms, there will be prerequisites for salvation. And no matter how minimal such prerequisites may be, they always shift the burden of proof of salvation from God to the individual.

For this reason Luther generally regarded all covenants with God negatively and preferred to emphasize God's testament to us. This emphasis is vividly expressed by Luther's discussion of inheritance rights and the certainty that a will provides the heir. Luther wrote,

A Testament, as everyone knows, is a promise made by one about to die, in which he designates his bequest and appoints his heirs. A Testament, therefore, involves, first, the death of the testator, and second, the promise of an inheritance and the naming of the heir. Thus Paul discusses at length the nature of testament in Rom. 4, Gal. 3 and 4, and Heb. 9. We see the same thing clearly also in these words of Christ. Christ testifies concerning his death when he says: "This is my body, which is given, this is my blood which is poured out" [Luke 22:19-20]. . . . He appoints and designates the heirs when he says "For you (Luke 22:19-20; I Cor. 11:24) and for many" (Matt. 26:28; Mark 14:24), that is, for those who accept and believe the promise of the testator. For here it is faith that makes men heirs, as we shall see. *(LW, 36, 38).

To emphasize his point, Luther said, "Let someone else pray, fast, go to confession, prepare himself for mass and the sacrament as he chooses. You do the same, but remember this is all pure foolishness and self-deception, if you do not set before you the words of the testament and arouse yourself to believe and desire them. You would have to spend a long time polishing your shoes, preening and primping to attain an inheritance, if you had no letter and seal with which you could prove your right to it. But if you have a letter and seal, and believe, desire, and seek it, it must be given to you, even though you were scaly, scabby, stinking and most filthy" (LW, 35, 88).

This image of God's testament clearly illustrates Luther's understanding of the radical response necessary to deal with insecurity. Sinners can bring nothing to God that will enable them to attain forgiveness—except their sin! Here Luther turned the medieval logic of salvation upside down, for in his thought the "unlike" is known by "unlike." The sinner does not ascend to God. Instead, God descends to the sinner. Fellowship with God is not achieved through improving and perfecting oneself through good works. Rather, fellowship with God is the gift of God apart from our works. Salvation does not depend on a change *within* us, that is, on our efforts to perfect our righteousness. Rather, salvation takes place *outside* us, that is, through the gift of God's righteousness to us. The radical message of the gospel is that it is the ungodly, the sinner, whom God accepts.

Luther used the image of marriage to illustrate this good news. Christ, the bridegroom, takes to himself the bride's sin, death, and damnation; and grace, life, and salvation become the sinner's. This arrangement is, Luther said, a "joyous exchange." "Who can understand the riches of the glory of this grace? Here this rich and divine bridegroom Christ marries this poor, wicked harlot, redeems her from all her evil, and adorns her with all his goodness" (LW, 31, 352).

Luther recognized the perpetual nature of the ambiguity and insecurity of personal and corporate life. As long as there is life on earth, there will never be life with security, that is, life without care, free from anxiety. All symbols of security are but fragile reflections of human efforts to construct a safe world.

The proper response to this frightening revelation is the recognition that no introspection and no outward activity can create the possibility of a secure life.

Luther saw that the root of the crises of his time was not rapid social change, immorality, lack of love, or personal and corporate corruption. To be sure, these are all serious problems that everyone should work to correct. But to assume that their correction will overcome the crisis of life is like assuming that rearranging the *Titanic's* deck chairs would have kept her afloat. The crisis of human life is overcome, not by striving to achieve security by what we do, but by the certainty of God's acceptance of us in spite of what we do. Luther never tired of proclaiming that the burden of proof for salvation rests, not on our deeds, but on God's action. This is good news indeed.

According to Luther, the source and focus of this good news is no longer our life and works but the proclamation and teaching of the gospel, what Luther called doctrine. "Doctrine and life must be distinguished. Life is bad among us, as it is among the papists, but we don't fight about life and condemn the papists on that account. Wycliffe and Huss [fourteenth-century critics of the papacy] didn't know this and attacked [the papacy] for its life. I don't scold myself into becoming good, but I fight over the Word and whether our adversaries teach it in its purity. That doctrine should be attacked—this has never before happened. This is my calling. . . . When the Word remains pure, then the life (even if there is something lacking in it) can be molded properly. Everything depends on the Word"(*LW*, 54, 110).

Doctrine over life! That claim is repugnant to many of us today because we pride ourselves on tolerance. But when life is placed over doctrine, the result is what Luther called the "monster of uncertainty."

> This monster of uncertainty is worse than all the other monsters. . . . It is obvious that the enemies of Christ teach what is uncertain, because they command consciences to be in doubt. . . .

Let us thank God, therefore, that we have been delivered from this monster of uncertainty and that now we can believe for a certainty that the Holy Spirit is crying and issuing that sigh too deep for words in our hearts. And this is our foundation: The Gospel commands us to look, not at our own good deeds or perfection but at God himself as He promises, and at Christ Himself the Mediator. . . . For I am clinging to God, who cannot lie. He says: "I am giving My own Son into death, so that by His blood He might redeem you from sin and death." Here I cannot have any doubts, unless I want to deny God altogether. And this is why our theology is certain: it snatches us away from ourselves and places us outside ourselves, so that we do not depend on our own strength, conscience, experience, person, or works but depend on that which is outside ourselves, that is, on the promise and truth of God, which cannot deceive (*LW*, 26, 386–87).

---

*All references in the form (*LW*, 00, 00) refer to *Luther's Works*, Helmut Lehmann and Jaroslav Pelikan, General Editors (Concordia and Fortress, 1955–87). The first number refers to the volume; the second number refers to the page.

[1] From *Manifestations of Discontent in Germany on the Eve of the Reformation*, edited and translated by Gerald Strauss (Indiana Universtiy Press, 1971); page 91.

[2] From *Manifestations of Discontent*; pages 91–92.

[3] From *Manifestations of Discontent*; page 96.

[4] From *Religious Poverty and the Profit Motive*, by Lester K. Little (Cornell University Press, 1978); page 38.

2

"Let God be God"—The Clue to Luther's Life and Ministry

In the first chapter of this book, we discussed Luther's environment as a world very much like our own. People experienced a great deal of insecurity and attempted to relieve that insecurity by acquiring righteousness before God. We saw that Luther's response was to reject all these efforts, not because he thought human righteousness could be better developed another way, but because he believed human righteousness is irrelevant before God. Because Jesus Christ came to save sinners, not the righteous, the only prerequisite for salvation is sin. This understanding of the gospel was liberating for Luther because he realized that it means that when we allow God to be God, we have the freedom to become what God intends us to be—human. Luther realized that we are not called to deny our humanity in efforts to become "like" God. Rather, the forgiveness of sin occurs in the midst of life. Put another way, salvation is not the goal of life that we must strive for but the gift that is the foundation of life.

Luther's Experience of Conversion

"Let God be God" is the clue to Luther's life and ministry. But as the term *clue* suggests, Luther did not reach this conviction without a tremendous struggle. As he himself said, "It is through living, indeed through dying and being damned that one becomes a theologian, not through understanding, reading, or speculation."[1] Luther's quest for certainty found its path in an experiential knowledge. He was not the first or the only person of his era for whom the usual tradition and practice of the church, conveyed by understanding, reading, or speculation, failed to bring peace and security to that most crucial crisis area of medieval life—one's relationship with God.

Luther's first steps on this quest for certainty in his relationship with God were not unlike those of many before him and countless others since—he entered "seminary." In Luther's case it was the Augustinian monastery in Erfurt. Again, not unlike countless other seminarians past and present, Luther's decision greatly upset his father. His father was by this time making a decent living at what we might call the medieval equivalent of working as a mining engineer. He had sent Martin to Erfurt University with the intention that Martin would earn a law degree, return home to Mansfeld, and perhaps even eventually become mayor of the city. But Luther's father's ambitious dreams were shattered by the same lightning bolt that knocked Martin to the ground as he walked back to Erfurt from his home town. In terror Martin had implored Saint Anne (the patron saint of miners) for help. He shouted, "I will become a monk!"

And become a monk Martin Luther did. In July of 1505, he entered the Black Cloister (the monks wore black) in Erfurt of the Observant Augustinians. Of all the monastic orders in Erfurt, this order was the most strict. The Black Augustinians were known for their rigorous pursuit of spiritual benefits. Their efforts more than matched in intensity the pursuit of material benefits Luther's father and other budding entrepreneurs practiced in the world. It was no less the business of monks to earn spiritual currency for

15

themselves and for others than it was the business of the early capitalists to earn material currency.

Luther threw himself wholeheartedly into the monastic regimen. Between the six worship services of each day, which began at 2:00 A.M., Luther sandwiched intense prayer, meditation, and spiritual exercises. But this regimen was just the normal routine for these monks. In his zeal to mortify his flesh and to make himself acceptable to God, Luther soon surpassed these practices. Luther subjected himself to long periods of fasting and self-flagellation. He spent many sleepless nights in a stone cell without a blanket to protect him from the damp cold that was characteristic of the area. Some scholars have suggested that these hardships all contributed to the continual illness that plagued Luther for the rest of his life. Later in life Luther said, "I almost fasted myself to death, for again and again I went for three days without taking a drop of water or a morsel of food. I was very serious about it"*(LW, 54, 339–40).

Luther was so serious about perfecting himself in order to receive acceptance from God that he became a burden to his fellow monks. The cause of this situation was the monastic practice of introspection and self-examination that probed and pried the conscience. The questions continually posed were, "Have I really done what lies within me? Have I really done my best for God?" No truly sensitive person under the pressure of striving to become holy can answer such questions affirmatively. Luther was in continual anxiety about his inability to achieve holiness. As a result, he constantly sought out spiritual guidance and confessors. Years later Luther remarked about all this: "Sometimes my confessor said to me when I repeatedly discussed silly sins with him, 'You are a fool. . . . God is not angry with you, but you are angry with God'" (LW, 54, 15).

Luther was indeed angry with God; so much so that he hated God. What Luther was experiencing was one of the two options that we experience when the burden of proof for salvation is thrown back on us—despair. The other option is pride, based on the assumption that we think we have definitely done enough to merit God's favor. But pride was not Luther's problem; despair and anger were.

Toward the end of his life, Luther reflected on this experience: "Though I lived as a monk without reproach, I felt that I was a sinner before God with an extremely distrubed conscience. I could not believe that He was placated by my satisfaction. I did not love, yes, I hated the righteous God who punishes sinners, and . . . I was angry with God, and said, 'As if, indeed, it is not enough, that miserable sinners, eternally lost through original sin, are crushed by every kind of calamity by the law of the decalogue, without having God add pain to pain by the gospel and also by the gospel threatening us with his righteousness and wrath!' Thus I raged with a fierce and troubled conscience. Nevertheless, I beat importunately upon Paul at that place, most ardently desiring to know what St. Paul wanted"(*LW* 34, 336–37).

"That place," of course, is Romans 1:17: "For in it [the gospel] the righteousness of God is revealed through faith for faith; as it is written, 'He who through faith is righteous shall live.'" But why did Luther hear the gospel as the threat of God's righteousness and wrath? The answer is that (as we mentioned in Chapter One of this book) medieval theology and pastoral care presented the righteousness of God as the standard sinners had to meet in order to be "like" God. No wonder Luther and many others thought of God as a wrathful tyrant, for they understood God's righteousness as a demand to be met. Years later Luther wrote, "But every time I read this passage, I always wished that God had never revealed the Gospel—for who could love a God who is angry, judges, and condemns?" (*LW*, 5, 158).

Luther's conversion occurred when he realized that we are not to think of the righteousness of God in the active sense (that we become righteousness like God) but rather in the passive sense (that God gives us his righteousness).

At last, by the mercy of God, meditating day and night, I gave heed to the context of the words, namely, "In it the righteousness of God is revealed, as it is written, 'He who through faith is righteous shall live.'" There I began to understand that the righteousness of God is that by which the righteous lives by a gift of God, namely by faith. And this is the meaning: the righteousness of God is revealed by the gospel, namely, the passive righteousness with which merciful God justifies us by faith, as it is written, "He who through faith is righteous shall live." Here I felt that I was altogether born again and had entered paradise itself through open gates. There a totally other face of the entire Scripture showed itself to me. Thereupon I ran through the Scriptures from memory. I also found in other terms an analogy, as, the work of God, that is, what God does in us, the power of God, with which he makes us strong, the wisdom of God, with which he makes us wise, the strength of God, the salvation of God, the glory of God (*LW*, 34, 337).

Luther's Expression of Conversion

Luther's conversion experience was not some sudden revelation that occurred to him one bright, sunny day in Wittenberg. As the above quotations make clear, his conversion was the culmination of long and intense study of the Scriptures. It did not come easily. His conversion was, as some scholars have suggested, a "language event." Luther's rediscovery of the good news came through his intense study of the language and grammar of the Bible. Whenever his conversion experience occurred (efforts to determine the precise date have been a favorite parlor game among Reformation scholars), it is at least clear that Luther's breakthrough came during his early years as Professor of Bible at the University of Wittenberg.

We mentioned that Luther entered the Augustinian

monastery in Erfurt in 1505. In the spring of 1507, he was ordained a priest. Four years later, partly as a means of reducing tensions within the Erfurt monastery and partly as a means of distracting Luther from his spiritual turmoil, he was sent to the new University of Wittenberg. While there, Luther was promoted to Doctor of Theology (1512) and immediately began lectures on biblical books—Psalms (1513), Romans (1515), Galatians (1516), Hebrews (1517). As anyone who has ever taught knows, having to explain something to others forces teachers to wrestle with the subject themselves. As Martin Luther himself put it, "[I] have become proficient by writing and teaching" (*LW*, 34, 338).

Write and teach he did! The good news that righteousness is the gift of God grasped Luther firmly. His energies were no longer consumed by constantly feeling his spiritual pulse and monitoring his internal growth in holiness. Once Luther realized that salvation was an event external to his own worthiness, he could turn his attention away from himself and outward to teaching and preaching this good news that the burden of proof for righteousness rests on God, not on us. An indication of both the power of Luther's message and the need that it met is the fact that the theology faculty of Wittenberg soon instituted a reform of the curriculum. In the spring of 1517, Luther wrote to his friend John Lang in Erfurt: "Our theology and St. Augustine are progressing well, and with God's help rule at our University. Aristotle is gradually falling from his throne, and his final doom is only a matter of time. . . . Indeed no one can expect to have any students if he does not want to teach this theology, that is, lecture on the Bible or on St. Augustine or another teacher of ecclesiastical eminence" (*LW*, 48, 42).

"'This theology" was not founded on religious experience or on personal holiness or on ethical perfection or on contributions to society or on any form of human achievement but only on the Word of God.

Aspects of Luther's Theology

We have belabored Luther's understanding of our righteousness before God (justification by grace alone through faith alone) because it is at the heart of everything Luther said and did after his conversion. At this point we need to take a moment to sketch out what difference this concept made in other aspects of Luther's theology.

The Reformation is sometimes described in terms of the watchwords *grace alone, Scripture alone,* and *faith alone.* We have already discussed what Luther meant by *grace alone.* But what did he mean by *Scripture alone* and *faith alone?* He did not mean by these battle cries what some modern Protestants mean when they use these terms. According to Luther, the Word of God is primarily Christ. Secondarily, the Word of God is the proclaimed or spoken Word. Luther was fond of emphasizing that faith comes by hearing the promise of God, for he was aware that we can look away from written words but have more difficulty "hearing away" from spoken words. Only on a third level did Luther relate the Word of God to the written words of the Bible. He firmly believed that the Word of God is not literally identical with the words of the Bible. The Bible is rather "the swaddling cloths and the manger in which Christ lies. . . . Simple and lowly are these swaddling cloths, but dear is the treasure, Christ, who lies in them" (*LW*, 35, 236).

Faith is our trust and confidence in God's promise, God's gospel. Faith is not belief in particular doctrines. Faith is a relationship with God, based on our trust in God. We are not saved by our faith but by God's grace. The tendency among Protestants to speak of "salvation by faith alone" can lead to the misunderstanding that our faith is something we do or believe. But holding that view would lead to understanding faith as a new kind of good work or merit. When we confuse faith with intellectual belief in particular doctrines or in biblical stories, then we are liable to fall into a kind of "can you top this" contest in which the person who can believe the most unbelievable things is considered to be the most Christian. This point of view is far afield from what Luther understood by faith: "Faith is not a paltry and petty matter. . . ; but it is a heartfelt confidence in God through Christ that Christ's suffering and death pertain to you and should belong to you" (*LW*, 22, 369).

Luther's radical understanding of justification brought with it a radical understanding of the person before God. Luther departed from all religious anthropologies that divide the person, whether it be into body and soul; body, soul, and spirit; flesh and spirit; or inner and outer. For Luther, the person is always the whole person. Luther could use traditional terminology, but he redefined it. Thus, in Luther's thought the distinction between *flesh* and *spirit* is no longer dualistic and anthropological but biblical and theological. The terms *flesh* and *spirit* do not designate parts of the person but refer to the whole person's relationship with God. "Flesh and spirit you must not understand as though flesh is only that which has to do with unchastity and spirit is only that which has to do with what is inwardly in the heart. . . .Thus you should learn to call him 'fleshly' too who thinks, teaches, and talks a great deal about lofty spiritual matters, yet does so without grace" (*LW*, 35, 371–72).

Human beings have no "higher power" or intrinsic capacity that entitles them to a relationship with God. The whole person is a sinner, not just some "lower" portion of the person. Sin is not doing bad things but rather not trusting God. "Unbelief is the root, the sap, and the chief power of all sin" (*LW*, 35, 369). In other words, the serpent's question to Eve is what each of us hears whispered in our own ears. Sin is the egocentric compulsion of the person to assert his or her own righteousness against God, the refusal to allow God to be God.

Acknowledgment of sin and the acceptance of God's judgment enable the sinner to live as righteous in spite of sin. By "letting God be God," that is, by ceasing one's efforts to be like God, the sinner is allowed to be what he or she is intended to be—human. The sinner is not called to deny his or her humanity and to seek "likeness" with God. Rather, the forgiveness of sins occurs in the midst of human life. The Christian before God, therefore, is at one and the same time righteous and sinful. The Christian "is at the same time both a sinner and a righteous man; a sinner in fact, but a righteous man by the sure imputation and promise of God that He will continue to deliver him from sin until He has completely cured him. And thus he is entirely healthy in hope, but in fact he is still a sinner" (LW, 25, 260).

The theological motif that relates justification and anthropology is the relationship of law and gospel. Luther moved beyond the traditional Augustinian concept of "spirit and letter" to his understanding of "law and gospel."

According to Luther, the distinction between law and gospel is the essential nerve of theological thinking; it is what makes a theologian a theologian. "Nearly the entire Scripture and the knowledge of all theology depends upon the correct understanding of law and gospel."[2] Throughout his career Luther never tired of emphasizing the distinction between law and gospel as the key to correct theology. He believed that it is only by making the proper distinction between law and gospel that human judgment and the Word of God may be distinguished.

The distinction Luther made between the law and the gospel is not a division or an "either-or" relation. Neither can replace or exclude the other. Law and gospel are not complementary. That is, the gospel does not need the addition of the law for fulfillment and vice versa. The law is not the gospel, and the gospel is not a new law.

This point brings us back to our earlier discussion of justification. The distinction between law and gospel is the distinction between two fundamental kinds of speech. The law is the communication of demands and conditions; it is the language of covenant. The law imposes an "If . . . then" structure on life. All law-type communication presents a future that is contingent on the person's works: "If you hold up your end of the bargain, then I will hold up mine." The gospel, however, is the communication of promise. It is the language of testament and has the pattern of "because . . . therefore": "Because I love you, I will commit myself to you." But even in the best of human relationships this analogy breaks down because there are all sorts of contingencies to our commitments over which we have no control. The clearest example, of course, is in our commitment to our children: Death may take us away just when they need us most. But we are not the gospel. The gospel is an unconditional promise because Christ made it. He has already satisfied all conditions, including death. In this sense, then, justification is not just a particular doctrine or item among others. Rather, justification by grace alone is *the* language that is always unconditional promise.

---

*All references in the form (*LW*, 00,00) refer to *Luther's Works*, Helmut Lehmann and Jaroslav Pelikan, General Editors (Concordia and Fortress, 1955–87). The first number refers to the volume; the second number refers to the page.

[1]From *D. Martin Luthers Werke*, Critical Edition (Hermann Böhlau); Vol. 5, page 163. [Lindberg's translation]

[2]From *D. Martin Luthers Werke*; Vol. 7, page 502. [Lindberg's translation]

3

The Rocky Road of Reformation

From 0 to 60 in Four Years

Luther was propelled into the public arena by the controversy over indulgences that began in the fall of 1517 as the result of his "Ninety-five Theses." Up to this time he had the "luxury" of pursuing his studies and developing his theology in company with his colleagues in the isolation of Wittenberg, a barren and muddy backwater town of about two thousand people. The word *luxury* is in quotes above because it was not as if Father Martin had nothing to do. He wrote to his friend Lang in October of 1516:

> I nearly need two copyists or secretaries. All day long I do almost nothing else than write letters; therefore I am sometimes not aware of whether or not I constantly repeat myself. . . . I am a preacher at the monastery, I am a reader during mealtimes, I am asked daily to preach in the city church, I have to supervise the study [of novices and friars], I am a vicar . . . (responsible for supervising eleven other monasteries), I am caretaker of the fish [pond] at Leitzkau, I represent the people of Herzberg at the court in Torgau, I lecture on Paul, and I am assembling [material for] a commentary on the Psalms. . . . I hardly have any uninterrupted time to say the Hourly Prayers and celebrate

[mass]. Besides all this there are my own struggles with the flesh, the world, and the devil. See what a lazy man I am!"*(*LW*, 48, 27–28).

However, as busy as Luther was, he still was able to choose his own issues. With the indulgence controversy this situation changed. His newfound opponents, not Luther, would pose the questions. As we will see, these issues led him further and faster in a direction he had never envisioned—the reform of the church.

The Indulgence Controversy and Its Aftermath

The concept of buying an indulgence to obtain God's favor should not be strange to us. A twist of the dials on our television sets on any given Sunday will bring us the modern, although somewhat paler, equivalent of the medieval indulgence seller. In general though, our modern media evangelists usually do not offer us much more than wealth and success in return for the money they request from us. The hard sell medieval indulgence seller such as John Tetzel, whom Luther opposed, offered much more: direct access to heaven for the souls in purgatory. One of Tetzel's famous little sales ditties was, "As soon as the coin into the box rings, a soul from purgatory to heaven springs!"(*LW*, 41, 232, Lindberg translation). Would you buy a used car from this man? Well, crowds of his contemporaries believed they were buying salvation from him. Tetzel was good at his job; but then he did get paid about one thousand dollars a month plus expenses, quite a large sum in those days.

Tetzel's routine would have been the envy of Madison Avenue had there been one at the time. His advance men announced his arrival some weeks before his visit to a town. They also compiled a special directory of the town that classified the financial resources of its citizens. When Tetzel arrived, it was with fanfare of trumpets and drums and a procession complete with flags and the symbols of the papacy. After preaching a vivid sermon in the town square on hell and its terrors, he would proceed to the largest church. He would then deliver an equally vivid sermon on purgatory and the sufferings not only awaiting his hearers but also those that dear grandma and other loved ones were already enduring. Finally, he would preach a sermon picturing heaven. At this point his audience was sufficiently prepared and eager to buy indulgences. Tetzel had something for everyone because he had a sliding scale of charges based on the person's financial resources.

Tetzel was not allowed to come into Wittenberg because Prince Frederick had his own relic collection with its indulgences and did not want competition. But Luther's parishioners overcame this inconvenience by going out to Tetzel. Luther was appalled when they returned and said they no longer needed to go to confession, penance, the Mass, and so forth because they now had a ticket to heaven.

This situation was the immediate context for the "Ninety-five Theses." In these theses Luther did not repudiate the doctrine of indulgences that said that the church can cancel the temporal punishments it has imposed in requiring acts of penance. What Luther attacked was the abuse of indulgences that was so evident in Tetzel's activities.

The popular image of Luther as an angry young man pounding his incendiary theses to the church door is far more fiction than reality. The "Ninety-five Theses" were a typical academic proposition for debate among scholars. They were written in Latin, and most Wittenbergers could not even read German. Then how did they create such an uproar? They were mailed, not nailed. Luther sent them to Tetzel's boss, Archbishop Albrecht of Mainz, with the naive thought that the archbishop did not know his hireling was abusing the authority of the church. Someone in the archbishop's office leaked the "Ninety-five Theses" to the press and sent them on to Rome. The result was an explosion that startled and frightened Luther as much or more than anyone else.

Luther had unknowingly touched the nerve of a far-ranging political and ecclesiastical scam. The pope, Leo X, was short of funds but wanted to build Saint Peter's in order to impress his secular rivals. Albrecht was legally too young to hold an archbishopric and was not even ordained, but he was of the ambitious House of Hohenzollern which was willing to put up the money to buy the post. The special papal dispensation that allowed Albrecht to become archbishop was based on his family paying a substantial amount of money. The sum was so large that the Hohenzollerns had to borrow it, at an exorbitant interest rate, from the famous Fugger banking house. The pope got his money, and we can now visit Saint Peter's. Archbishop Albrecht was given the right to sell indulgences in order to pay back the huge loan. No wonder it was a hard sell!

Events accelerated rapidly for Luther. In the summer of 1518, the pope's theologian, Sylvester Prierias, informed Luther that he was a heretic for attacking the authority of the church. Interestingly, the initial issue of the Reformation was not justification by grace alone but the authority of the church, specifically that of the papacy. Luther wrote, "Presently Sylvester . . . entered the arena, fulminating against me with this syllogism: 'Whoever questions what the Roman church says and does is heretical. Luther questions what the Roman church says and does, and therefore (he is a heretic).' So it all began"(LW, 54, 265).

Within months Luther was ordered to go to Rome, but local pride and German law saved him. Prince Frederick realized that student enrollment had increased markedly at the university he had founded in Wittenberg not so long before. He was not about to let his prize professor and academic drawing card go off to be burned at the stake. Besides, German law said its citizens should be tried in its own courts.

Arrangements were made to have Luther interviewed by papal representatives in Germany, but the outcome was unsatisfactory. At his meeting with Cardinal Cajetan in Augsburg in October 1518, Luther would not recant; and the cardinal would not discuss the issues.

The next major step in what was rapidly becoming the "Luther affair" occurred in a debate in Leipzig in July 1519. Surrounded by colleagues and armed students, Luther journeyed to Leipzig. The university there was the rival of Wittenberg's. In Leipzig, Luther confronted one of the most vicious and clever debaters of the time, John Eck.

Eck prodded Luther with charges that he was a Hussite and Bohemian, charges tantamount in that context to being called a communist in the 1950's in the United States. Luther protested but after some consideration burst out that many of the condemned articles of the Hussites were indeed Christian and evangelical and should not have been condemned. The audience was shocked. Eck pressed on, and Luther finally asserted that both the papacy and church councils may err. Eck had scored an immediate triumph; and Luther was face to face with the implication of the teachings he had been developing over the last years: Christ alone is head of the church. This understanding was the reason Luther began to call the papacy the Antichrist. Luther's focus was not on the notorious morality of the Renaissance popes but rather on the papal institution's usurpation of the place of Christ.

Luther was now on center stage. Within a year the papal bull *Exsurge Domine* ("Arise, Lord," June 24, 1520) was published in Rome. Luther was given sixty days to recant or be excommunicated with all his followers. If he failed to recant, his very memory in the minds of people was to be erased. That was easier said than done, however, for much of Germany had already rallied to Luther's side.

When the bull was posted in Germany, it was defaced. When the book burnings that normally accompanied such a bull took place, gleeful students lugged papal and scholastic works out of the libraries to give to illiterate enforcers of the bull to burn instead. Eck himself added fuel to the fires by adding his own private "enemies list" to the bull's list of those condemned.

The sixtieth day of grace the bull granted to Luther fell on December 10, 1520. On that day Luther's university colleague Melanchthon led the faculty and students out of the University of Wittenberg for a truly revolutionary act. They pubicly and solemnly burned the constitutional foundations of medieval Europe: the books of canon and civil law. Luther himself threw the papal bull on the fire. After singing the *Te Deum*, the faculty returned to the university. The students carried on demonstrations against the pope for the next few days until the town authorities stopped them. The actual bull of excommunication, *Decet Romanum*, was published on January 3, 1521.

The papacy then urged Emperor Charles V to issue a mandate against Luther, but the German constitution and Charles's coronation oath upholding the right of Germans to be tried by an impartial panel of judges stood in the way. The political solution was to guarantee Luther safe passage to the Diet, or German parliament, meeting in Worms in the spring of 1521. Luther's popularity is illustrated by the experience of Aleander, the papal representative, upon his arrival in Worms. He could not find a comfortable room, people threatened him in the streets, and the bookstores were full of Luther's writings.

Luther's friends warned him that a century earlier John Huss also had been given a safe conduct (to the Council of Constance) but was then burned as a heretic. Rumors also abounded that Luther would be abducted and killed. Nevertheless, Luther made his way to Worms. There before the emperor, princes, and lords—a whole world away from his monastic cell and dingy classroom—Luther did not receive the hearing he expected. Instead, he was presented with a pile of his writings and asked whether he was the author and whether he wished to retract their errors. His brief answer included the memorable lines, "Unless I am convinced by the testimony of the Scriptures or by clear reason (for I do not trust either in the pope or in councils alone, since it is well known that they have often erred and contradicted themselves), I am bound by the Scriptures I have quoted and my conscience is captive to the Word of God. I cannot and I will not retract anything, since it is neither safe nor right to go against conscience. I cannot do otherwise, here I stand, may God help me, Amen" (*LW*, 32, 112–13).

The evening the Diet closed, the emperor gathered a rump Diet (a legislature having only part of its original members) of conservative princes and bishops and issued the Edict of Worms. Luther was not only excommunicated, he was declared to be an outlaw. All people were forbidden to have any dealings with Luther and were ordered to seize him and deliver him to the authorities. Luther's followers and supporters were to be treated likewise. Their property was to be confiscated and given to the person carrying out the edict.

On Luther's way back to Wittenberg he was kidnaped by orders of his own prince, Frederick the Wise, and taken in secret to the prince's Wartburg Castle. Luther was kept there in protective custody disguised as a knight for nearly a year (early May 1521, to early March 1522).

The Wittenberg Disturbances

A new theology had been proclaimed. Many people welcomed it, and there was increasing pressure for applying it to the church. But Luther had disappeared, and rumors of his death were rampant. Since Luther was not in Wittenberg, the leadership of the new movement fell on the shoulders of his colleague Karlstadt. A brief overview of the situation in

Wittenberg reveals the storms Karlstadt had to face. Karlstadt was about to receive the ministerial equivalent of a battlefield commission.

A ground swell of popular clamor for immediate reform was very much in evidence, but we should not mistake the volume of this clamor for its size. Many people did not want to change the old ways. One of the most important of these people was the prince himself. He was concerned about outside intervention if things in Wittenberg got out of hand. "Agitators" came to Wittenberg from Zwickau, a town already torn by religious riots over the new theology. Known as the "Zwickau prophets," these men seriously disturbed both clergy and laypersons by claiming they had received apocalyptic visions and had heard voices from God. These people also prophesied an imminent Turkish invasion and the consequent end of the world. They claimed that Scripture is not sufficient, for people are to be taught by the Spirit alone. "Inside agitators" were also present in Wittenberg. The monk Gabriel Zwilling, who regarded himself as a second Luther, disrupted the Augustinian monastery and successfully urged many monks to depart. To add to the troubles, students began to leave the university because of the intrusion of spiritualism.

As all these storm clouds were breaking over Wittenberg, Luther was in the Wartburg. He was chafing over his confinement but throwing himself into his work. During this period Luther translated the New Testament from Greek into German. This masterful and still influential translation was potentially more revolutionary than manning the barricades, for it was the first step toward universal education and the deprivation of the elite of exclusive control over words as well as over the Word.

The Invocavit Sermons

Luther arrived in Wittenberg on Friday, March 6, 1522. The following Sunday, Invocavit (the first Sunday in Lent), he began a series of sermons that lasted for the rest of the week. His theme was the distinction between an evangelical "may" and a legalistic "must." Luther emphasized that faith active in love gives us patience for the neighbor who is not equally strong in faith. He said that his concern was not with the reforms themselves but with their haste and with the fact that people were being forced to accept them. Luther noted that the sacrifice of order and the consequent offense to the weak resulted from making a "must" out of what is free. Faith is a free gift. No one can be forced to have it. Certainly, Luther opposed the papists; but he thought that one should do so only with God's Word and not with force. He said, "I will constrain no man by force, for faith must come freely without compulsion. Take myself as an example. I opposed indulgences and all the papists, but never with force. I simply taught, preached, and wrote God's Word; otherwise I did nothing. And while I slept . . . or drank Wittenberg beer with my friends Philip and Amsdorf, the Word so greatly weakened the papacy that no prince or emperor ever inflicted such losses upon it. I did nothing; the Word did everything"(LW, 51, 77).

Luther argued that forced reform changed the good news into bad news, that is, the gospel into law. The history of the church shows, he argued, that one law quickly leads to thousands of laws. Furthermore, rushing about smashing altars is counterproductive, for it only sets images more firmly in persons' hearts. Only God's Word can truly capture our hearts. The reformers could also create the suspicion that they were flaunting their Christian liberty in order to show their superiority. Luther wrote, "For if you desire to be regarded as better Christians than others just because you take the sacrament into your hands and also receive it in both kinds, you are bad Christians as far as I am concerned" (LW, 51, 91).

Luther's sermons differentiated reformation from puritanism. He thought that the abolition of clerical abuses and the forced institution of reform, no matter how correct the theology, did violence to ignorant and unconvinced consciences. The weak need to be started on pablum and then gradually led to the strong meat of Christian freedom. To do otherwise would be to reform only outward things. The effect of these sermons was an almost immediate restoration of order. Innovations ceased for the time being and so did the violence.

We know confrontation was not alien to Luther. His stances before Cardinal Cajetan in Augsburg and the emperor in Worms were both confrontational. Yet, he knew, in a way that others did not, that confrontation is never the first word in the practice of Christian discipleship. Unless grounded repeatedly in God's Word of forgiveness and acceptance, discipleship too easily becomes *our* words and *our* programs. The startling aspect of Luther's translation of theology into the practice of ministry is that in the midst of personal and social disintegration, he did not tell people what they ought to do but rather what God had done for them. Luther's approach is startling because as causes get underway or as things come apart, our natural inclination is to admonish people and to try to force them to accept our views. Luther knew that in time of crisis the Christian approach is clear proclamation of the Word.

---

*All references in the form (*LW*, 00, 00) refer to *Luther's Works*, Helmut Lehmann and Jaroslav Pelikan, General Editors (Concordia and Fortress, 1955–87). The first number refers to the volume; the second number refers to the page.

4

The Christian Life: Word and Sacraments

The Church as the Communion of Saints

We concluded our last chapter with Luther's emphasis on the proclamation of the gospel. His conviction was that faith comes by hearing. "So faith comes from what is heard, and what is heard comes by the preaching of Christ"(Romans 10:17). Luther even defined the church as a "mouth house." According to Luther, the church is that community that is constituted by the Word, by speaking the gospel. He wrote, "Thank God, a seven year old child knows what the church is, namely, holy believers and sheep who hear the voice of their Shepherd. So children pray, 'I believe in the one holy Christian church.' Its holiness . . . consists of the Word of God and true faith."[1]

Luther's point here is that the unity and marks of the church are not institutional structures or even the like-mindedness of the members of the community but the proclamation of the gospel—the unconditional promise of God embodied in Word and in sacrament. The organization of the church exhibits the same life as the church's members: a life (lived in the shadow of the cross) that is simultaneously sinful and righteous. Therefore, the church as an organization, like its members, lives by the continuous encounter with the Word of God and will be constantly in process of reformation. The church is dynamic, not static. In other words, the church is not defined by the character of its members but rather by the primary characteristic of the assembly—the preaching of the gospel. This is the basis on which the church stands or falls. "If we lose the doctrine of justification, [for Luther, the heart of the gospel] we lose simply everything. Hence the most necessary and important thing is that we teach and repeat this doctrine daily"*(LW, 26, 26). The church too is an article of faith. It is identified by the visible signs of the preached Word of God and by the "visible Words" of baptism and the Lord's Supper.

We will soon explore further Luther's understanding of the Lord's Supper. However, at this point we need to see that his understanding of the Lord's Supper as Communion relates to his understanding of the church as the "communion of saints." One of Luther's greatest achievements in reform was the rediscovery of the church as community. In fact, Luther disliked using the term *church* (*Kirche*) because of its association with organization and buildings. He much preferred the term *community* (*communio, Gemeine*). In his *Large Catechism*, Luther wrote that the word *ecclesia* properly means an assembly. "We, however, are accustomed to the term *Kirche*, 'church,' by which simple folk understand not a group of people but a consecrated house or building. But the house should not be called a church except for the single reason that the group of people assembles there. For we who assemble select a special place and give the house its name by virtue of the assembly."[2]

The Life of the Community

Luther did not just remain at the level of theological theory concerning the church. He strove to assist the life of the community through the development of worship services, instruction, and art. With the conviction that "there is much that is Christian and good under the papacy" (*LW*, 40, 231), Luther retained the basic liturgical forms of medieval worship. The changes he instituted were designed to promote a clearer proclamation that it is God who justifies the ungodly through Christ.

Luther's liturgical reforms proceeded with the same sure touch for language and common sense that made his German translation of the Bible so influential. At the same time, Luther insisted that the main purpose of worship is the right proclamation of the gospel and the administration of the sacraments. Luther was remarkably free from either an antiquarian interest in restoring ancient rites or a zeal for "baptizing" current fads. A mark of his impressive grasp of the essentials of worship is the fact that his reforms became a pattern for worship that people still experience in Lutheran churches today around the world.

The Eucharistic Controversies

Luther believed that Word and sacrament are both integral to worship. Following Augustine, Luther understood the Lord's Supper as the "visible Word" and therefore no less the Word of God than the Bible readings and the sermon. Therefore, God is really present for our salvation in the Lord's Supper as well as in the proclaimed Word. This conviction led Luther into a two-fronted struggle against both the medieval understanding of the Lord's Supper in terms of transubstantiation and other Protestant understandings of the Lord's Supper as merely symbolic and a memorial of Jesus Christ's death. The sixteenth-century Eucharistic controversies are a complicated topic which we will be able to grasp more easily if we approach them by asking what difference one or another particular theological interpretation made to Luther.

Luther rejected the medieval theology of transubstantiation. He believed that in practice it led to a nonevangelical emphasis on merit gained by performing the rite, concentrated spiritual and political power in the clergy, and created superstition among the people. The first reason was the crucial one. Transubstantiation, the actual changing of the bread and wine into the body and blood of Jesus Christ by the priest, was considered to be the reoffering of Jesus Christ's death to God. The assumption was that we are confronted by an angry God who is appeased by and rewards our offering him his Son. The multiplication of altars in medieval churches, still evident in their architecture today, indicates how widespread this idea was. However, the sixteenth-century reformers did not accept that point of view. If there was one thing the reformers agreed on, it was that the Crucifixion was the once and for all atonement for our sins. God's self-sacrifice for us cannot be repeated by us, and repetitive masses are not meritorious for our salvation.

In practice the sacrament was understood in the medieval church as a transaction with God carried out by priests. Therefore, participation by the congregation was not necessary. Luther's theology of the Lord's Supper reinstituted it as Communion, an event celebrating the living relationship between God's promise and our faith. The Lord's Supper is a communciation event that establishes the fellowship of the congregation. Again, the theme here is Luther's tireless insistence that the burden of proof for salvation rests on God, not on our works. Thus, the Mass should be understood, not as a sacrifice, but as a testament.

The medieval understanding that the priest "makes God" on the altar was a key to the great spiritual and political power of the medieval church. The priest had the power to cut people off, to have them excommunicated, not just from the church, but from God. Such power was open to the abuse of ecclesiastical tyranny over the community.

The dogma of transubstantiation also led to fear and superstition among the laity. The practice of giving only the bread in Communion came from the fear of the laity that they might spill the wine, Jesus Christ's blood. Bread is more manageable; people can catch or sweep up the crumbs. Furthermore, since the bread is Jesus Christ's flesh, people believed that it contained his blood also. Hence the origin of stories about evil persons stealing the consecrated host and breaking it, only to be drowned in the blood that poured forth from the bread.

Where many contemporary Protestants have difficulty with Luther's theology of the Lord's Supper is in regard to his insistence that Christ is really present in the bread and wine. Luther clearly desired to retain the Roman Catholic concept of Christ's presence, which lies behind the doctrine of transubstantiation. However, Luther rejected transubstantiation because he saw this doctrine as a philosophical attempt to explain *how* God is present. Luther believed that the point of the Lord's Supper is not explanation but proclamation—the proclamation that God really is present here *for us*. In other words, God is as present in the sacrament as in the proclaimed gospel.

Luther's main Protestant opponent on this point was Ulrich Zwingli, the reformer of Zurich, Switzerland. In 1529, Luther, Zwingli, and their respective colleagues met in Marburg, Germany. They wanted to hash out their differences. These reformers agreed on fourteen of fifteen items. The item they did not agree on was the Lord's Supper.

Zwingli insisted that the Lord's Supper is a symbolic memorial wherein we remember Jesus Christ's atoning death. Luther's response was that in the sacrament as in the proclaimed gospel, no prerequisite on our part is assumed. That is, God is truly present offering us forgiveness and salvation whether we believe it or not, whether we have done good works or not, whether we have a heartfelt remembrance of encountering Jesus Christ or not. Once again, for Luther the burden of proof is always on God, not on us. If we say that worthy participation in the Lord's Supper depends on our state of mind, then we have usurped God's prerogative of claiming us and are instead advancing a claim on God. Some people say that the infrequency of Communion in some Protestant churches is a consequence of the idea that we must be worthy before communing. Luther's helpful insight expressed in his doctrine of the real presence is that the only prerequisite to salvation is sin—only sinners may be justified.

Ministry: Proclamation Over Model

Luther applied his insistence on the reality of the gospel in Word and sacrament apart from any merit or worthiness of persons to the clergy as well as to the laity. God's Word is not dependent on the worthiness of the preacher. We all, clergy and laity alike, are to strive to live in conformity with Christ. But the fact that we are all sinful as well as righteous does not invalidate the gospel. This point may seem obvious, but it needs emphasis because Protestants tend to understand their minister's role as that of being a model of the godly life. Such a misunderstanding is what lies behind difficulties faced by pastors, their spouses, and their children and is the source of the whispers that end with "and *he* (or *she*) is a minister!" According to Luther, the pastor is primarily proclaimer of the Word and administrator of the sacraments, not the model of a godly life. Luther's position, which Augustine first forcefully set forth in his controversy with the Donatists, should be of comfort to pastors. As one of my seminary professors once remarked, "If God can speak through Balaam's ass, he can speak through you too!"

The Catechisms

As proclaimer of the Word, the pastor is also responsible for instructing the community. Among the tools that Luther provided for this responsibility are his *Small Catechism* and his *Large Catechism*, both of which appeared in 1529. The catechisms originated in a series of sermons that Luther had been preaching on the Ten Commandments, the Apostles' Creed, and the Lord's Prayer.

The *Small Catechism* was a doctrinal handbook for the laity and for children. Along with brief explanations of the Ten Commandments, the Apostles' Creed, and the Lord's Prayer, Luther included short expositions of baptism and the Lord's Supper, an instruction for confession, morning and evening prayers, and grace for meals. Luther presented these materials in the form of short questions and answers intended to teach faith and to encourage moral and spiritual improvement.

The *Large Catechism*, intended for the instruction of pastors and heads of households, treats each of the sections of the *Small Catechism* in greater detail but without losing its simplicity and direct address to our human needs and concerns. As any teacher seasoned with the professorial syndrome of saying more and more about less and less knows, simple exposition of complex subjects is no mean feat.

Luther's Life: Facets of Faith

Luther felt that faith in God's grace liberated him from oppressive striving to please God and others and freed him to be himself—warts and all. The first of the theses in his tract "The Freedom of a Christian" reads, "A Christian is a perfectly free lord of all, subject to none." (The second, complementary thesis, "A Christian is a perfectly dutiful servant of all, subject to all," will be the subject of our next chapter.) Luther's freedom to be human, evident not least of all in his sense of humor, was based on his understanding of (read "standing under") faith. "Faith is a living, daring confidence in God's grace, so sure and certain that the believer would stake his life on it a thousand times. This knowledge of and confidence in God's grace makes men glad and bold and happy in dealing with God and with all creatures" (*LW*, 35, 370–71).

When viewed through the eyes of faith, creation everywhere bears witness to God's gifts. Luther frequently commented that we are surrounded by miracles to which we pay no heed because they seem so commonplace. "If the stars did not rise during every single night or in all places, how great a gathering of people there would be for this spectacle! Now not one of us even opens a window because of it" (*LW*, 1, 127).

Closer to home is the creation of new life. "When the fetus has been brought into the world by birth, no new nourishment appears, but a new way and method: from the two breasts, as from a fountain, there flows milk by which the baby is nourished. All these developments afford the fullest occasion for wonderment and are wholly beyond our understanding, but because of their continued recurrence they have come to be regarded as commonplace, and we have verily become deaf to this lovely music of nature" (*LW*, 1, 126).

A keen observer of the lessons of nature, Luther frequently commented about his dog, affectionately named Clumsy Oaf (*Toelpel*). Seeing his dog's riveted attention when begging for a scrap, Luther commented, "Oh, if I could only pray the way this dog watches the meat! All his thoughts are concentrated on the piece of meat. Otherwise he has no thought, wish, or hope" (*LW*, 54, 38). On another occasion Luther recounted with great delight the story of a "Lutheran" dog. "Once when there was a procession with banners around a church, the verger put the holy water pot on the ground. A dog came along and [urinated] into the holy water pot. A priest noticed this because he was sprinkling the water, and he said, 'You impious dog! Have you become a Lutheran too?'"(*LW*, 54, 421).

Perhaps *the* subject on which Luther contributed insights yet to be realized by many of his heirs in the faith is sexuality. To Luther, sex and marriage were a glimpse of what the lost Eden must have been like. Certainly he knew that married life was not one long honeymoon. He commented that if we knew what lay in store for us, we probably would not get married.

41

But he vigorously criticized vows of celibacy because they removed men and women from service to the neighbor, contravened the divine order of marriage and the family, and denied the goodness of sexuality. Luther viewed marriage as not just the legitimation of sexual fulfillment but as above all the context for creating a new awareness of human community. "Marriage does not consist only of sleeping with a woman—everybody can do that!—but keeping house and bringing up children" (*LW*, 54, 441). Luther was fond of extolling marriage as a "gift of God, . . . superior to any celibacy, [for] the companionship of husband and wife is a marvelous thing."[3]

Luther knew firsthand the pain of the loss of children. His daughter Elizabeth died in infancy. "There is no sweeter union than that in a good marriage. Nor is there any death more bitter than that which separates a married couple. Only the death of children comes close to this; how much this hurts I have myself experienced" (*LW*, 54, 33). His daughter Magdalene died in his arms when she was only thirteen. "It's strange to know that she is surely at peace and that she is well off there, very well off, and yet to grieve so much!" (*LW*, 54, 432).

Luther married his Katie in 1525 "to spite the pope!" (*LW*, 29,21). Yet, his correspondence with his wife reveals a remarkable relationship of faith and love. Luther had not wanted to get married, for he was an outlaw and was convinced that he would be put to death. But Katherine von Bora was a runaway nun who with others had escaped to Wittenberg. The others were soon married off (a single woman had few possibilities in the Middle Ages), but Katherine rejected several offers while hinting strongly she would rather marry Martin. Besides, his father wanted grandchildren. So, Luther married her. Soon he stated, "I wouldn't give up my Katie for France or for Venice" (*LW*, 54, 7). She was, he said, God's gift to him. They had six children whom they loved dearly and with whom Luther enjoyed playing. He also liked to entertain them with fables and music.

Katie was an indispensable part of Luther's family life. He was on the road a lot, and on one of his trips he wrote to Katie that he could find nothing to buy to bring home for the children. So, he asked her to have something special for him to give to them when he returned.

Katie nurtured and scolded Luther through more than twenty-five years of what certainly must have been one of the most eventful marriages in history. Luther was convinced that God had come to his aid by giving him a wife. By Luther's account Katie was, among other things, the best brewer of beer in Wittenberg.

Luther's appreciation for creation, astonishing in light of both medieval and far too many modern attitudes, was rooted, as was all his life, in Romans 1:17: "He who through faith is righteous shall live." To Luther this "living" was not to be put off until heaven. He reversed the medieval warning of death that in the midst of life we are surrounded by death and made it a call to life by affirming that in the midst of death we are surrounded by life.

---

*All references in the form (*LW*, 00,00) refer to *Luther's Works*, Helmut Lehmann and Jaroslav Pelikan, General Editors (Concordia and Fortress, 1955–87). The first number refers to the volume; the second number refers to the page.

[1]From "The Smalcald Articles," by Martin Luther, in *The Book of Concord: The Confessions of the Evangelical Lutheran Church*, edited and translated by Theodore G. Tappert (Muhlenberg [now Fortress] Press, 1959); page 315.

[2]From *The Large Catechism*, in *The Book of Concord*; page 416.

[3]From "The Truth About Luther's Marriage," by Rudolf Thiel, translated by Gustav Wiencke, in *The Lutheran Church Quarterly*, Vol. XIX, January, 1946; page 89.

5

The Christian Life: Being Christ to the Neighbor

Luther's thesis that "a Christian is a perfectly dutiful servant of all, subject to all"*(LW, 31, 344) succinctly captures the theme of our responsibility for the world. Up to now we have focused on Luther's emphasis on God's gifts to us of righteousness, forgiveness, mercy, love, and, above all, the gift of God himself. Luther retained this emphasis when he talked about Christian responsibility and servanthood to others. Luther's remarks about Christian works were always in terms of vocation. *Vocation* is derived from a Latin word that means to call, to invite, to welcome, to call by name. Christian vocation is not primarily our works but our being called by name and welcomed by God to be "a perfectly dutiful servant of all." Therefore, love of the neighbor is not separated from love and worship of God.

Vocation

Luther's contribution to a Christian understanding of work was to place work within the context of vocation or calling. This approach was a major break from medieval tradition. Prior to Luther the word *vocation* was reserved for the specific religious life of priest or monk or nun. Luther's emphasis that every baptized Christian belongs to the priesthood of believers freed *vocation* from its narrow religious definition. Luther freed us to wrestle with the fact that our vocation is not outside the sphere of everyday life but is precisely in the midst of everyday life.

This concept is just one more way of saying that every aspect of life is anchored in the forgiveness of sins. Luther emphasized that when we let God be God, we are free to become human. What this point of view means for our vocation is that we are not called to serve God outside the world, we are called to serve our neighbors in the world. The good news that our righteousness, our worth as persons, is not dependent on what we do but on who we are releases energy that would otherwise be directed into "religious" activity.

We live in a culture that ranks our value as persons according to our jobs. We are constantly receiving materialistic messages from our culture that tell us that "you are what you eat," "you are what you do." Luther's recovery of a gospel understanding of vocation says, to the contrary, "You have worth because God is calling you."

God does not call us out of the world but into its midst. Because our acceptance by God occurs on the human level, we are not called to extraordinary tasks but to the mundane arena of everyday life. English does not communicate this concept as vividly as does Luther's German. In German, the vocabulary of religion and everyday work are closely tied together. The words for gift and word are incorporated in the words for duty and responsibility. *Gabe* means gift, and *Aufgabe* means duty. Thus, the word *duty* carries within it the element of gift. Vocation is not divorced from God but clearly reflects God's gift. The same is true in the relations of the German words *Wort* (word), *Antwort* (answer), and *Verantwortung* (responsibility). In all three, the Word is present. Thus, the Word of God calls forth our answer, which in turn encompasses our everyday responsibilities. Our works express our faith.

The Gospel: The Compass to Vocation

All analogies break down at some point, but it may be helpful to think of the gospel as a compass rather than as a map to our vocation. The gospel does not provide us with a road map but serves us as a compass. A map is limited to a particular area and presents us with specific roads and paths to follow. A compass, however, expands our horizons. It does not limit us to a particular road. A compass allows us the freedom to relate in all directions, to all areas of life. Our vocation then en*compasses* all our relationships: son or daughter, brother or sister, mother or father, spouse, neighbor, citizen, student, teacher, worker, or retiree. We live in a web of relationships, the many strands of which are anchored in the center of the forgiveness of sins. We practice our vocation in these relationships of life. This fact means that there is a "God-givenness" to life that is specific to the particular relationships and talents each of us have.

Our vocation comes to us in the concrete circumstances of our lives. Thus, God is pleased when we carry out the duties these circumstances assign to us. But we always think we know better. We strive to go beyond the tasks given to us just as the medieval person thought it would be holier to be a priest or nun than to be a farmer or a wife. We dream and we struggle to do something special—the big thing, the extraordinary thing. This kind of goal orientation leads to the neglect of the relationships already at hand. That fact is the reason Luther chose examples of vocation from everyday life: The maid sweeping the floor; the mother washing diapers; the brewer making beer. These activities are all concrete forms of service to the neighbor. Indeed, our specific relationships and skills are a kind of mini-Bible, teaching us how to fulfill our vocation. Unfortunately, as Luther clearly saw, most of us see these tasks as drudgery or as irritating inconveniences that prevent us from doing important things.

However, God's forgiveness of sins frees us from the self-imposed burden of trying to bring in the kingdom of God. In less theological terms, we need the ability to "let go" or, as Luther put it, "to let God be God" (*LW*, 31, 10). We Americans especially have the tendency to think that what we do has ultimate significance. We are very goal oriented. Luther's understanding of vocation in light of the forgiveness of sins allows us to say that we have done all we can.

Trusting God in this way is, of course, a difficult thing to do. But there is no virtue in trying to solve everything ourselves. There is sufficient evil in every day; we do not need to borrow more. The world will not collapse if we are not superparent, superspouse, or superworker. If we have the confidence that God upholds us, we will be able to do our work faithfully rather than neurotically.

On the other hand, an understanding of vocation in the context of the forgiveness of sins will guide us beyond disappointments and despair. Some of us fall into cynicism when we realize that some problems are not ultimately resolvable. We tend to trim our ethics when we see other people being successful without being faithful. As the writer of Ecclesiastes said, "So I turned about and gave my heart up to despair over all the toil of my labors under the sun, because sometimes a man who has toiled with wisdom and knowledge and skill must leave all to be enjoyed by a man who did not toil for it" (2:20-21a). Luther's point, however, is that we are not called to be successful; we are called to be faithful. What we do is significant whether we are successful or not because we are witnessing to the kingdom of God. "If God were to order you to polish the shoes of the devil or the worst rogue, you would have to comply. And this work would be just as good as the greatest work of all, because God orders you to do it. Therefore you should have no regard for any person in this matter, but you should regard only what God wants. Then the most insignificant work, if it is done properly, is better in the sight of God than the works of all the priests and monks put together" (*LW*, 30, 83). Our vocation should not be goal oriented but source oriented.

Guidelines in Vocation

But how are we to know what God wants? How are we, as Luther put it, to be "little Christs" to our neighbors? The clue to Luther's answer is in his distinction between law and gospel. We live out our vocations in the context of the structures provided by God's law and on the basis of the forgiveness of sins. This situation was never an abstraction to Luther. As he said, everything in our workshops calls out to be used in service of the neighbor.

This arrangement is certainly simple, but it is not casual. We live in a structured universe in which life has a certain givenness. We serve best when we develop our talents in accordance with this givenness. We faithfully use our knowledge of life when we realize that our neighbor is not helped if we lend him or her a ladder with rotten rungs. Similarly, a person may be imbued with all faith to serve his or her neighbor in medicine; but if this person is "all thumbs," most of us would prefer a competent atheist to take out our tonsils. Or, as Luther expressed this point with regard to government, "It is not necessary for the emperor to be a saint. It is not necessary for him to be a Christian to rule. It is sufficient for the emperor to possess reason."[1]

When we are aware of our own strengths and weaknesses, we are better able to serve our neighbor. The old story of the farm boy illustrates this point. Looking at the clouds one day, he saw the letters *P.C.* He thought they meant "preach Christ." After a difficult year in seminary, someone suggested that the letters might better be interpreted to mean "plant corn." The point is that we are to develop our own aptitudes. Each of us is in a particular situation related to our environment and heredity. For Christians, this situation is not a deterministic grave but a cradle for development. We are born into situations to be grappled with, not into patterns to be filled out. These situations occur in our everyday lives. On this basis we can develop competence in something. By doing so, we will not only derive satisfaction but will also have something with which to serve our neighbors.

A Dutiful Servant of *All*

Luther's understanding of the Christian life was by no means limited to personal vocation. To him, Christian vocation was social as well as personal. Service to the neighbor occurs not only when we feed the hungry, clothe the naked, visit the sick and prisoners, and release captives. This service occurs when we work to change the social structures that contribute to hunger, nakedness, homelessness, and imprisonment. Luther's involvement in and contribution to this subject may be clearly seen in three areas: education, social welfare, and politics.

Education

Luther and other reformers were intensely interested in education because they wanted everyone to be able to read the Bible. Their concern was the beginning in our culture of the emphasis on universal, public education for girls as well as for boys.

In 1524, Luther published a tract titled "To the Councilmen of All Cities in Germany That They Establish and Maintain Christian Schools." In this tract he maintained that education is not only necessary for the spiritual growth of boys and girls but is also essential if they are to become good citizens.

Luther also advocated the establishment of public libraries: "Finally, one thing more merits serious consideration by all those who earnestly desire to have such schools and languages established and maintained in Germany. It is this: no effort or expense should be spared to provide good libraries or book repositories, especially in the larger cities which can well afford it. . . . Indeed, all the kingdoms which ever amounted to anything gave careful attention to this matter" (*LW*, 45, 373).

Luther's advice was not without success, for within the next two years a number of major cities took action on it. However, Luther continued to be disturbed by the fact that many parents were more interested in their children making money than in their children learning to serve society. So, in 1530, he published another tract, "A Sermon on Keeping Children in School." Here he again argued that it is absolutely necessary for society that the youth be educated. Indeed, having educated youth is even more important for society than for the church because God will care for the church; "but in the worldly kingdom men must act on the basis of reason—wherein the laws also have their origin" (*LW*, 46, 242). "I hold that it is the duty of the temporal authority to compel its subjects to keep their children in school . . . so that there will always be preachers, jurists, pastors, writers, physicians, schoolmasters, and the like, for we cannot do without them" (*LW*, 46, 256).

Social Welfare

Luther was also quite concerned about social welfare. His society faced extensive and often severe poverty. Pre-Reformation laws to compel able-bodied beggars to work were largely ineffective because the medieval church had developed an ideology of poverty as a virtue. The poor person was presented as blessed by God and as an object for the meritorious work of almsgiving. That is, the wealthy earned merit for salvation by giving alms. In short, poor people were understood to be part of God's plan of salvation; God provided them for the benefit of the rich.

Luther's rejection of charity as a means of salvation undercut this ideology of poverty. Since salvation is a free gift apart from works, the need no longer exists to have poor people as objects for the practice of charity.

Thus, Luther and other reformers attacked both the idea that poverty is a virtue and the social roots of poverty. Luther's response to this social issue was his development of the "common chest," a forerunner of the United Way.

Nearly every town that adopted the Reformation enacted legislation that included provision for this common chest. The common chest was literally a large chest kept in the town's main church and locked with four different locks. The chest contained the church funds, offerings, and account books. An elected representative from each quarter of the town had a key to one of the locks. Every Sunday these representatives and the church deacons met to assess the needs of the town's poor people and to provide for distribution of money and goods to them. The funds of the common chest were for immediate assistance to the poor, provision of low interest loans for poor workers and tradespersons, subsidy of education for the children of the poor, and provision of dowries for daughters of the poor. The legislation establishing the common chest was concerned not only with such remedial relief work but also with developing social structures and policies, such as job training, to try to prevent poverty.

Politics

These brief examples of Luther's efforts to establish and maintain education and social welfare programs indicate he was no stranger to politics. He was convinced that good government does not just happen but is rather the result of that service to all neighbors that takes education and reason seriously.

Luther's dialectic of law and gospel was the theological basis for his vigorous distinction between the kingdom of God and the kingdom of this world. He hammered so incessantly on this distinction because he wanted to call Christians to political action in an age that conceived of religion as withdrawal from the world. People in medieval Europe could not think of a "vocation" in the world because politics was "dirty business," and the word *vocation* had a narrow religious interpretation. By distinguishing between righteousness in the world based on works and righteousness before God based on grace, Luther hoped to free Christians for service in a world always shrouded in political ambiguity. "This is our theology, by which we teach a precise distinction between these two kinds of righteousness, the active and the passive, so that morality and faith, works and grace, secular society and religion may not be confused. Both are necessary, but both must be kept within their limits" (*LW*, 26, 7).

According to Luther, the identification of any political program, regardless of its intrinsic merit, with the gospel is to subvert both politics and the gospel. The political process is subverted because ambiguity and compromise have no place in claims to absolute righteousness. National self-righteousness soon moves to brand political opponents as followers of the Devil. The gospel is subverted because it becomes the norm to which all citizens are to be forced to conform. The gospel is no longer the free gift of God when salvation is presented as dependent on a particular political affiliation and program.

Luther understood himself to be a theologian, not a politician. His political insights were grounded in his understanding of the gospel. People need his political realism today as much as they did in the sixteenth century. We too need to be reminded that salvation is not attainable by political programs. At the same time, we need to be reminded that political programs may indeed be vehicles for serving our neighbors. According to Luther, faith alone grants us the security to live within the human insecurity of relative political structures. Only by faith can we avoid the defensive sanctification of past, present, or future goods and values. Faith is the enabling ground of the person who is content to be human and to let God be God. In other words, the Christian is to take seriously the task of maintaining and building up society but with the conviction that every culture, every system of justice, and every political structure is only relative and instrumental for the humanization of persons. Reason and love are to be active in the continual task of socialization but with the recognition that God, not the party or the church, is sovereign in history.

Luther died in Eisleben in 1546, following his successful mediation of a political dispute between the counts of Mansfeld. He had lived out to the end his understanding of vocation. Some years before his death, Luther had preached, "This life indeed is transitory, a voyage and pilgrimage to our true home. But God wills that while we are here we should serve our neighbors through our respective callings. Thus we will do what is imposed on us and truly serve our subjects, neighbors, spouses and children while we can, even if we know we must leave this earth this very hour. For, praise God, even if we should die now, we know where we belong, where our true home is. But since we are still on our way, we shall and will do what belongs to our earthly citizenship. And thus we shall live among others according to the laws of this place even up to the hour when we shall cross the threshold. Thereby we shall travel with honor and leave no complaint behind."[2]

---

*All references in the form (*LW*, 00, 00) refer to *Luther's Works*, Helmut Lehmann and Jaroslav Pelikan, General Editors (Concordia and Fortress, 1955–87). The first number refers to the volume; the second number refers to the page.

[1]From *D. Martin Luthers Werke*, Critical Edition (Hermann Böhlau); Vol. 27, pages 417–18. [Lindberg translation]

[2]From *Dr. Martin Luthers Sämmtliche Schriften*, edited by J. G. Walch (Lutherischer Concordia-Verlag, 1883); Vol. 12, pages 570–71. [Lindberg translation]

6

The Reception of Luther

We have discussed Luther's life and ministry, and we have seen that Luther insisted that every aspect of life is related to God's good news of the free forgiveness of sin. How were Luther and his emphasis on the gospel received? Did people recognize his rediscovery of the gospel as valid? Did the church make the conversation Luther initiated a part of its faith and life? That is, did the church recognize Luther's lively give and take conversation about the gospel to be in full harmony with the apostolic faith?

The answers to these and similar questions vary with the concerns and times of the persons asked. In his own time people pictured Luther as either an angel or as a devil. During the evangelical awakening in England, Wesley attributed to Luther the spark for his own conversion experience but also blamed him for an abysmal ignorance of sanctification. We know too that, historically, Luther's call for reform of the church led to its division. And yet, some Roman Catholic scholars today receive Luther as a "father in the faith." The conversation that Luther began has continued down to the present. Indeed, this conversation has been so lively that lengthy studies have been written just on the reception of Luther.

In this chapter we will first look briefly at how Luther's contemporaries received him. Doing so will give us the context in which to discuss the Roman Catholic responses to Luther as they took shape in the work of Ignatius Loyola and at the Council of Trent. We will conclude with a discussion of Luther's reception by people today and his legacy to the churches.

Luther's Reception by His Contemporaries

We have already suggested that there were few, if any, nonpartisan responses to Luther in his time. After Pope Leo X's initial dismissal of the indulgence controversy as another quarrel among drunken German monks, the members of the religious establishment became increasingly aware that they could not ignore Luther. Rather, the church was faced with having either to receive and recognize Luther's interpretation of the gospel as apostolic or to reject it as heretical. From the first official papal response to the "Ninety-Five Theses" by Sylvester Prierias in 1518 up to the 1930's, the predominant Roman Catholic reaction to Luther was nonreceptive. The reaction was that conversation cannot be held with an archheretic.

One of the persons most influential in perpetuating an image of Luther designed to poison ecumenical conversation was not a pope or even a famous theologian but Luther's contemporary John Cochlaeus (1479–1552). Cochlaeus's first writing against Luther, *Septiceps Lutherus* (1529), set out to show the contradictions in Luther's thought. Cochlaeus divided Luther's work into seven periods from which apparently contradictory selections from Luther's writings were drawn. The book itself is a masterpiece of tedium and distortion. Its impact is due to the genius of the anonymous artist who designed the cartoon on the title page. This drawing shows a seven-headed monstrous Luther with each head in conflict with every other head.

Three years after Luther's death, Cochlaeus published his much more influential work titled *Commentary on the Acts and Writings of Martin Luther* (1549). In the most excessive terms Cochlaeus attributed the Reformation to Luther's evil lust, subjectivity, and ambitions, which Cochlaeus explained by the story that Satan created Luther. In 1943, Adolf Herte, a German Roman Catholic professor, published a three-volume study that traces Cochlaeus's influence on Roman Catholic Luther scholarship up to the early twentieth century.

While Luther was being vilified by Cochlaeus, Luther's own followers after his death went to the opposite extreme by describing him in biblical imagery. Melanchthon set the tone when, upon hearing of Luther's death, he compared Luther to the prophet Elijah. Others soon compared Luther to Jeremiah, John the Baptist, and Moses!

Neither Heretic Nor Saint

Luther did not regard himself as either a heretic or a saint. His ability to respond vigorously, even roughly, to opponents who attacked his understanding of the gospel is well-known. However, the fact that Luther rejected with comparable vigor efforts during his lifetime to raise him to special status is not as well-known. For example, in 1522 Luther attempted to diffuse the widespread unrest and growing resentment against the church through his pamphlet "A Sincere Admonition by Martin Luther to All Christians to Guard Against Insurrection and Rebellion." In this writing Luther stated,

> I ask that men make no reference to my name; let them call themselves Christians, not Lutherans. What is Luther? After all, the teaching is not mine [John 7:16]. Neither was I crucified for anyone [I Cor. 1:13]. St. Paul, in I Corinthians 3, would not

allow the Christians to call themselves Pauline or Petrine, but Christian. How then should I—poor stinking maggot-fodder that I am—come to have men call the children of Christ by my wretched name? Not so, my dear friends; let us abolish all party names and call ourselves Christians, after him whose teaching we hold. . . . I neither am nor want to be anyone's master. I hold, together with the universal church, the one universal master. I hold, together with the universal church, the one universal teaching of Christ, who is our only master [Matt. 23:8] *(LW, 45, 70–71).

However, many of the churches rooted in Luther's reform movement came to call themselves Lutheran. Some Lutheran churches, however, mainly outside North America, have recognized Luther's point and refer to themselves as "evangelical" or as "of the Augsburg Confession" (to indicate their reception of Luther's interpretation of the gospel as expressed by his followers in the city of Augsburg in 1530).

The Augsburg Confession

The Augsburg Confession summarizes faith and identity for the churches that arose from Luther's reform movement. Luther did not write this document. It was the product of his colleague and friend Philip Melanchthon, a layperson. The Augsburg Confession lists in twenty-one articles what the signers confessed to be the essentials of the Christian faith and then adds as a supplement some of the abuses in the church of their day that they felt needed correction. The document immediately achieved significance as a public declaration of faith because it was presented to the emperor at the Diet of Augsburg. He had requested a statement of Protestant beliefs. Seven princes and the representatives of two free cities had signed it.

The signers of the Augsburg Confession were, as they stated in its preface, presenting "a confession of our pastors' and preachers' teaching and of our own faith, setting forth how and in what manner, on the basis of Holy Scriptures, these things are preached, taught, communicated, and embraced in our lands, principalities, dominions, cities, and territories."[1]

True to Luther's understanding of the church as the community characterized by the preaching of the gospel, Article VII of the Augsburg Confession presented an ecumenical expression of the church: "It is also taught among us that one holy Christian church will be and remain forever. This is the assembly of all believers among whom the Gospel is preached in its purity and the holy sacraments are administered according to the Gospel. For it is sufficient for the true unity of the Christian church that the Gospel be preached in conformity with a pure understanding of it and that the sacraments be administered in accordance with the divine Word. It is not necessary for the true unity of the Christian church that ceremonies, instituted by men, should be observed uniformly in all places."[2]

The members of the religious establishment did not receive the Augsburg Confession positively. In fact, it was countered two days later at the Diet of Augsburg itself by the "Roman Confutation," drafted by a commission of theologians headed by the papal legate. The Counter Reformation had begun.

The Roman Catholic Reformation

We spoke above of the Counter Reformation, but now as our subheading we have used the phrase "Roman Catholic Reformation." This phrase is not intended to create confusion but rather to indicate that the sixteenth-century Roman Catholic Church was engaged not only in efforts to "counter" Luther and other Protestant leaders but was also engaged in positive efforts for renewal, evangelization, and mission. These frequently dual engagements are highlighted in the contributions of the founder of the Jesuit Order, Ignatius Loyola, and in the institutional response of the church itself through the Council of Trent.

Ignatius Loyola

In his person, Loyola (1491–1556) was the embodiment of both traditional Roman Catholicism and the Counter Reformation. The youngest of twelve children born to a Basque family of noble lineage, Loyola was trained from his youth in the ideals of the nobility that, it should be noted, were not always ideal or noble. Although he was much taken by romances of chivalry, his life as a courtier was far from edifying. While it may be too strong to characterize his life in royal courts and in barracks as dissolute, it is not too strong to say that his life took an abrupt about-face as the result of his volunteering to help defend the city of Pamplona against an advancing French army.

During the battle a cannonball broke his right leg and wounded his left. A doctor in the victorious French army set Loyola's leg, and he was taken back to the family castle. The doctors there found that the leg had been set badly. Loyola insisted that the leg be rebroken and reset and that a protuding bone be sawed off! The ensuing discomfort and nine months of convalescence gave Loyola time for reflection about his life. Influenced by the reading available to him in the castle, a book on the life of Jesus Christ and a book on the lives of the saints, Loyola came to the conviction that God wanted him to become a spiritual knight. In March of 1522 on the feast of the Annunciation at the shrine of the virgin Mary at Montserrat, he offered up his sword and, as he put it, clothed himself "with the armor of Christ."[3]

Loyola spent the next year in ascetic retreat, living in a cave near Manresa, a town outside Barcelona. His notes and reflections on this period of rigorous introspection formed the basis for his later famous and influential *Spiritual Exercises*. Although not published until 1548, this guide for developing conformity to God's will was already in use in 1527.

The *Exercises* were designed to guide a person through a thirty-day retreat of religious experience. The systematic reasoning and meditation of the *Exercises* included daily self-examination that focused on cultivating a single virtue or on attacking a single sinful inclination. This approach allowed one problem area after another to be conquered in the intended process for reform of the person's life. Loyola's key to reform of the church was the reform of individuals. The problem of the church as Loyola saw it was not doctrinal aberration, as Luther believed, but rather personal aberration from doctrine and from the institution.

We do not have space to sketch the interesting and eventful years of Loyola's ministry to reform and renew the church. But we cannot go on to discuss the Council of Trent without saying a few words about that last major medieval monastic order, the Jesuits. In 1540, Pope Paul III approved the life of service to the church that Loyola and his small group of companions envisaged.

The Society of Jesus was a distinct development from the older monastic orders of the church. Loyola's emphasis on action in the world replaced the older monastic ideal of contemplation and withdrawal from the world. This emphasis on the active life required well-educated priests, which, in turn, led to the well-known long and rigorous training required of candidates for the Society. The extra training was to interiorize monastic discipline (to make it part of one's own inner being) because the Jesuits were not to be isolated in a monastery but active in the world in mission and in evangelism. Another distinctive element of the Society of Jesus was that the candidate for membership took not only the three regular religious vows of poverty, chastity, and obedience but also a fourth vow: a special vow of obedience to the pope.

This special fourth vow of obedience to the pope starkly highlights Loyola's difference from Luther on reform. To Loyola the church was the hierarchical church. Loyola had no interest in reforming its structure, worship, and theology. His understanding of reform was personal, not institutional. Loyola's understanding of reform was the epitome of the Council of Trent's papalism.

The Council of Trent

Loyola's understanding of reform animated the Council of Trent. His concept of individual renewal as the key to church renewal and the fact that members of the Society of Jesus played key roles in the council as papal theologians made quite an impact. The council, as did Loyola himself, illustrated the twin concerns of the Roman Catholic Church: self-renewal and opposition to what the church regarded as Protestant heresy. The council was convened in 1545 in a theoretically still-united Christendom. The council closed in 1563 in a Christendom rent by divisions that still affect us today.

From almost the very beginning of the Reformation, Luther had called for a "free, Christian council" to resolve doctrinal conflicts and to reform the church. Papal reluctance to agree to such a council was rooted in political as well as in theological concerns. The conciliar movement of the fifteenth century had strongly challenged papal authority when it tried to place the pope under the authority of councils. And Luther's call for a free, Christian council meant a council free of papal domination, informed by the Scriptures. The long delay in convening this council also related to the fact that the members of every party wanted the council to meet in their own territory so they could control it for their own advantage. The town of Trent in northern Italy was finally chosen because it was technically on German soil and therefore appeased the emperor. For a variety of political reasons we cannot explore here, the council did not actually meet for the whole period 1545–63 but in three assemblies: 1545–47, 1551–52, and 1562–63.

The agenda for the council was heresy and reform,

and the council decided to debate these concerns simultaneously. The constitution of the council departed from that of previous councils by granting votes to individuals rather than to national church representatives. This arrangement gave the papacy an advantage because of the predominant number of Italians at the council.

Although the council did not condemn Luther in a formal, judicial sense, the doctrinal decisions of the council were intended to counter the Reformation. Against the Reformation watchword of *Scripture alone*, the council put forth the position that Scripture *and* tradition are the two sources for Christian truth. The significance of this decision is that the Magisterium, the teaching authority of the Roman Catholic Church, is the interpreter of tradition and, therefore, of Scripture. This decision was complemented by the decree that made the Vulgate, the old Latin translation of the Bible, the official text of the Bible. In response to the Reformation watchword of *grace alone*, the council affirmed the role of human cooperation with grace. In response to the Reformation emphasis on baptism and the Lord's Supper as the two sacraments of the Christian faith, the council affirmed seven sacraments.

The papacy, which Luther attacked with increasing bitterness toward the end of his career, registered a major triumph at the council. Indeed, the council became a papal means for a renewed rejection of conciliarism (the theory of church government that puts final authority in the hands of representative ecclesiastical councils rather than in the hands of the papacy). Another council was not held for three centuries! And when Vatican I met in 1869–70, the primacy and infallibility of the pope were made explicit.

The Council of Trent acknowledged the calls for reform by both Roman Catholic and Protestant reformers in the area of the life of the church, not in its doctrine. Disciplinary decrees of the council called for emphasis on preaching based on Scripture and the establishment of seminaries to provide an educated clergy for preaching and pastoral care. A variety of moral reforms were also set forth with regard to clerical celibacy and chastity and with regard to the residency and faithfulness of bishops.

As we have mentioned above, the Roman Catholic reform movement was essentially personal. The church was to be transformed by transforming its members, hence the importance of Loyola's and the Council of Trent's emphasis on personal, spiritual renewal. But this renewal of prayer, penance, and works of mercy, as important as it was, neglected liturgical reform. The heroic stature of individuals such as Ignatius Loyola could not substitute for the centrality of public, corporate worship which Luther and other Protestant reformers had recovered. In the face of the Reformation's emphasis on corporate worship, Communion, and hymnody, the Council of Trent and the Roman Catholic reform remained liturgically indifferent. Only in our own time is the Roman Catholic Church incorporating some of Luther's contributions to worship.

Luther's Legacy to the Churches

Textbooks on the Reformation frequently conclude with a chapter that discusses the legacy the modern world inherited from the Reformation. These chapters examine the many ways Luther's initial religious quest influenced every aspect of modern culture: education, politics, philosophy, art, science, economics, music, and literature. This information is all quite interesting, but what would Luther see as his legacy to the churches?

I think that if Luther were asked to name only one thing he could bequeath to future generations, he would want it to be his fundamental proposal of the gospel in the radical sense of justification by grace alone apart from *all* works, be they ethical, psychological, or emotional. All that Luther did, he did as a minister of the church—the church that is recognizable wherever the gospel of the unconditional promise of God is unconditionally proclaimed. Luther's legacy to the churches, to us, is his joyous discovery and affirmation that the gospel includes no ifs, buts, or maybes but rather affirms our destiny without any conditions. "The Gospel commands us to look, not at our own good deeds or perfection but at God Himself as He promises, and at Christ Himself, the Mediator. . . . He says: 'I am giving My own Son into death, so that by His blood He might redeem you from sin and death.' Here I cannot have any doubts, unless I want to deny God altogether. And this is the reason why our theology is certain: it snatches us away from ourselves and places us outside ourselves, so that we do not depend on our own strength, conscience, experience, person, or works but depend on that which is outside ourselves, that is, on the promise and truth of God, which cannot deceive" (*LW*, 26, 387).

---

*All references in the form (*LW*,00, 00) refer to *Luther's Works*, Helmut Lehmann and Jaroslav Pelikan, General Editors (Corcordia and Fortress, 1955–87). The first number refers to the volume; the second number refers to the page.

[1]From *The Book of Concord: The Confessions of the Evangelical Lutheran Church*, edited and translated by Theodore G. Tappert (Muhlenberg [now Fortress] Press, 1959); page 25.

[2]From *The Book of Concord*; page 32.

[3]From "Ignatius Loyola," by Robert E. McNally, S.J., in *Reformers in Profile*, edited by B. A. Gerrish (Fortress Press, 1967); page 237.